GEMS C

Inspiring Words from Sri Swami Satchidananda

Integral Yoga® Publications
Yogaville, Virginia

<u>Gems of Wisdom</u> was excerpted from these books by Sri Swami Satchidananda:

Beyond Words

To Know Your Self

The Golden Present

Integral Yoga® Publications
Satchidananda Ashram - Yogaville
Buckingham, Virginia 23921 USA

DEDICATION

This booklet is lovingly dedicated to our beloved Master, H.H. Sri Gurudev Swami Satchidanandaji Maharaj, on the auspicious occasion of Guru Poornima 1988.

Sri Gurudev's teachings are true gems of wisdom and even a single one of them sincerely applied will bring great achievement in every area of life. The sayings here are selections on a particular subject. For more in-depth study, the seeker may read any and all of Sri Gurudev's books.

This booklet, though small in size, is certainly jewel-like in its quality. May each of us who reads and reflects upon these words come closer to reflecting that gem-like quality that is our True Nature.

COMMEMORATION

This booklet is also dedicated in loving memory of Smt. Jayamani Dharmalingam in commemoration of the one-year anniversary of her Jalasamadhi.

ACKNOWLEDGEMENTS

We gratefully acknowledge those who helped in the preparation of this booklet:

Swami Premananda Ma, Swami Hamsananda Ma, Swami Sharadananda Ma, Kumari Margid and Uma Knight.

DISCIPLINE

Many people fear that discipline means a lack
of freedom, a repression or joyless life.
Without discipline over our mind, where is the
joy? With that control you can enjoy any thing
you want. Nothing is dangerous to you then.

*

If you can keep control over the mind, wherever
you are will be a heaven. If you do not have
that control, even if you are in heaven, it will
be a hell for you.

*

The greatest victory you can win is the victory
over your own mind.

*

Discipline makes your mind stronger and one
-pointed. It should ultimately help you make
your mind your slave.

*

Don't be controlled by anything. Exercise your
mastery. That is the aim of Yoga.

*

Don't ever forget that any achievement in life
is based on discipline.

*

It is through your discipline and meditation
that you are being cleared and opened up to

receive the true essence within.

✳

Keep the mind clean, the body clean, the life well disciplined, the heart dedicated. This is Yoga.

✳

Speak less and only speak about what is to be spoken of. Control of the tongue is very important. The tongue does two things: tasting and talking. Have limitations in both.

✳

You will enjoy the world when you know how to handle it well, when you become master of it.

✳

A yogi is like a surfer who knows how to balance on his board. He welcomes even a big rolling wave because he knows how to enjoy it without getting caught in it.

✳

There should be a tranquility in everything, a limitation in everything. Then you will see that your life is completely transformed.

FAITH

Trust in God and fear do not go together.

✳

If you have complete faith, nothing is impossible.

✳

If there is one quality a seeker must have, it is unshakable faith.

✳

If you have faith, you don't need to worry about anything; you will be given the strength to accept everything.

✳

If you have absolute faith, you will always be happy and joyful, even in the midst of suffering.

✳

The sign of a good devotee is complete faith in God's Will. To accept both pleasure and pain, profit and loss, praise and blame, equally as God's gift. Whatever comes, accept it as God's Will.

✳

Resign yourself completely into the hands of God, into the hands of the unseen power that functions through you. You will be contented.

If you believe in God, you know that God gives you everything that you need and takes away everything that you don't need.

✳

If you really give yourself completely in the hands of God, you don't have to worry about anything.

✳

God is there to take care of everything, every minute.

✳

Just have faith.

✳

Difficult situations come to give us a chance to prove our trust in a Higher Energy.

✳

Without faith, nobody can become a spiritual seeker.

GOD

God is really everywhere, not in a particular form, but as an omnipresent awareness or power. God is consciousness itself.

✳

Put God first. That is the first and foremost thing to achieve. God is the only reality. All the rest is a dream.

✳

To a real spiritual seeker, God is the only buddy.

✳

Know that you are being guided by God. Whatever situation is presented to you is presented by God. You should realize that.

✳

Serving God is loving God.

✳

God is in you in the form of peace and joy.

✳

God does not help from the outside. He is within you. When you are pure, you reflect that Godly quality. When you have made the mind calm and clear, you express that divinity.

✳

Your conscience is that part of God that is within you.

Trust in God; then all of life will be joyful and peaceful.

*

The ultimate help comes from the God within.

*

It doesn't matter what you do, your goal should be to come closer to this understanding: "Essentially I am God's spirit, I am the pure Self. I am Existence-Knowledge-Bliss Absolute."

*

The only real help comes from God.

*

The more you trust God, the more you will get tested. Trust and testing go together.

*

Lord, it's all Your name. It's all Your form. It's all Your deed. And it's all for good.

*

You are never alone. God is nearer than your own heart.

*

If you want God to come in, make room.

THE GURU

The Guru is one who eliminates or removes the darkness in your understanding.

✳

The Guru's inspiration, the Guru's force, the Guru's divine energy, the Guru's vibration will always be there guiding you, directing you.

✳

The Guru's purpose is not simply to say, "You are wonderful." A Guru is simply a laundryman. He is trying to wash the dirty laundry.

✳

The <u>teaching</u> is the real teacher. If you follow the teaching, you will always have the teacher with you.

✳

Don't try to get the teacher into your heart; instead, get the teaching into your heart. Keep it there, and you will feel your master's presence and guidance always.

✳

A Guru will not force anything into you. He will wait until you ask, until you become ready.

✳

Imparting knowledge is not normally done with words. Speaking through silence, in feelings,

will help you receive more than through
words.

*

The Guru is not a person somewhere. Your
conscience always tells you what is right and
what is wrong. That is the Guru within. Listen
to that, and follow it.

*

Even if you don't have a Guru, even if you have
no one to advise you, if you learn to listen
within, your own conscience will guide you.
The Guru has gone the route. He knows the
journey and is able to guide others on the trip.
That is the duty of the teacher. But you have
to follow the teaching, and there is no short-cut
on this road.

*

The Guru is not really bringing you anything
new; instead he or she is simply removing the
obstacles so the flow of consciousness will be
continuous and the water can reach its source.

*

The entire nature is the omnipresent Guru.
Draw silent lessons from all around you.

HAPPINESS

Everything and everybody is looking for happiness. But it is not something that has to be brought in from outside. Happiness is already within us and is to be experienced.

✳

You are happiness personified.

✳

Real freedom is enjoying whatever you do.

✳

Who will be the happiest person? The one who brings happiness to others.

✳

Happiness is in you. If you take care not to lose it, it is always there.

✳

No one can ever give you happiness or unhappiness, but only reflect or distort your own inner happiness.

✳

There is nothing in this world that will make you always happy.

✳

Pleasure and pain come together; they are part of this world. Let your happiness be something that is above pleasure and pain.

Without peace, nothing is going to make you happy. If you have peace, even without having anything else, you will be happy.

＊

Don't depend on something that comes from outside. Outside things are never going to make you happy. And it <u>should</u> be that way, so that one day you will realize that there is always someone to love and comfort us inside.

＊

If you want to be happy, work for the happiness of all people everywhere.

＊

The best remedy for any illness is laughter.

＊

Real bliss is maintaining equanimity of mind at all times, at all places, under all circumstances.

＊

Your own true nature is happiness. The minute you realize that you are always happy, that you have a permanent relationship within, then you become independent. You don't depend on anything or anyone for your happiness.

HEALTH AND HEALING

The human body is a temple. Keep it strong and supple. To purify the body practice the disciplines of hatha yoga and take care of your diet.

※

There are three conditions that food should meet: it should help your mind maintain its tranquility; it should not stiffen the body with toxins; and it should be able to be digested quickly without wasting a lot of energy.

※

To become a good instrument of the Divine, maintain your health - have an easeful body, a peaceful mind and a useful life.

※

The body and the mind are interconnected and interdependent. The body expresses the thoughts of the mind. If you have a happy mind, your face and body will reflect that happiness.

※

The sign of a healthy person is being happy and relaxed anywhere and everywhere. A really healthy person takes everything in life as a game.

The worst fear is the fear of death. When your old clothes wear out, you throw them away and put on new ones. <u>You</u> were never born and <u>you</u> are never going to die. <u>You</u> are ageless; only the body has age. The soul is immortal.

✳

If you believe in God, if you trust God wholeheartedly, even your sickness will go away because you are putting yourself into the hands of a more powerful doctor.

✳

Believe that you can draw healing energy from the Divine by clean living.

✳

If you have total faith in a Higher Will - a Higher Energy - you will be able to tune in to that and receive all the strength and energy to recharge your system.

✳

Health is your birthright, not disease. The person with health and strength of body, soundness of mind, with morality and spirit, is a real gem among all humanity.

LOVE

Real love is possible only when you see everything as an expression of yourself.

✳

Love has no boundaries; it is the greatest force on earth.

✳

Show the same love to one and all. Let nothing get harmed, hurt, or pained, even by your thought.

✳

Love misplaced or used improperly can bring wars, can cause crimes.

✳

Love has a great purpose. It should go up and up -- until you learn to love your neighbor as your own Self. Make a resolution not to bring any harm to anybody by using your love in an improper way. Let your love bring good to everybody.

✳

You do not need to be doing great things. In your own small way, among your neighbors, around your house, see that you are a friend to everyone. Learn to love everyone equally, no matter what he or she is.

Concern about the feelings of others and the happiness of others is real love.

✳

Love is concern for others, doing good to everyone and everything. Utilize your love for the benefit of the Creation.

✳

If you want to experience that in your life, love everything and everybody as God would love: unconditionally.

✳

We lose trust and become miserable when love is conducted like a business. If your relationship is based on some gain from that person, you are never going to be happy. Be content just to love.

✳

True love knows no bargains. It is one way traffic: giving, giving, giving.

✳

The whole world exists in love. We come with love and we go with love. And in between we live with love. Love is the basis of everything.

✳

Love for the sake of love because that love makes you happy. That happiness cannot be taken away by anybody.

MANTRAM AND MEDITATION

Spend a few minutes each day in meditation.
These are the most important minutes you can
spend. You will be able to send out nice,
peaceful vibrations, and these vibrations will
go around the globe.

*

When the mind is totally focused on your object
of concentration, then that one thought is also
dropped and the mind becomes naturally
vacant.

*

Even when you are physically doing something,
your aim can be meditation. Focusing your
entire mind on what you are doing is
meditation.

*

To have the proper attunement, the mind
should be one-pointed and free of selfish
motives.

*

Repetition of a mantram, a spiritual sound
vibration, is the simplest and best practice for
concentration.

*

The mantram is your protection and a shield
around you. Wear the mantram as your armor.

There is no greater power than that.

✳

By repetition of a mantram alone, many hundreds of great saints have experienced Divine Consciousness.

✳

Knowing the meaning of the mantram is not even necessary. The faith behind it is more important.

✳

Receiving mantra initiation is like having a beautiful seed planted within you. It is your duty to water it, to see that it gets enough nourishment and that no wild weeds grow up.

✳

Whatever mantram is given to you, or whichever one you choose, stick to that one and have complete faith in it.

✳

Repeat the mantram consciously until your system takes over and repeats it unconsciously. Very soon you will realize how happy and healthy and peaceful you can be.

MARRIAGE

True marriage means you don't expect anything
from the other partner. You marry someone else
to give all that you can.

✳

The true purpose of a marriage is to give, not to
ask for anything for yourself.

✳

Realize that you don't have a relationship to
be happy. You are already married to your
peace and joy.

✳

If you are getting into a matrimonial
relationship with someone, know that you are
having somebody to offer all your services to.
Don't expect anything in return from that
person. Both of you should think that way.
Such a marriage will last.

✳

Real marriage is when two people agree on one
goal or purpose in life.

✳

As husband and wife you are two but you should
see as one. The two minds are the two eyes. You
should have one goal and toward that goal you
should both go like the two wings of the same
bird or two oars of the same boat.

True spiritual marriage is when the husband's and wife's love for each other blends together and becomes the love of God.

✳

Living together happily as one beautiful family with total love is God.

✳

If you come together to be partners in living a dedicated life, a life of service, then the marriage will be made in heaven.

✳

The true spiritual marriage is a wedding between two reflections of God.

✳

Serve the Divinity reflected in your partner.

✳

We are all married to one another in spirit.

✳

There is a pretty young man or young woman always with you: the peace within. You are wedded to that. Let us not disturb it or divorce it to get someone else.

PEACE

The ultimate quest of the entire world is peace.
Only in peace do we have joy.

*

Our first and foremost duty is to take care not to
let the mind lose its peace.

*

Stay away from anything that disturbs your
peace, from anything that will bring
disappointments, anxieties and worries.

*

Peace, contentment, not running after anything
is what you call the kingdom of God.

*

Absence of turmoil is not real peace. Real peace
is when you rise above the turmoil and stay
peaceful in the midst of it.

*

Peace can be maintained when all your actions
are free from selfish motives.

*

It is not in renouncing actions that you will find
peace, but in renouncing your attachment to the
results of the actions.

*

Nothing from outside can give you peace
because peace is there in you, always.

Your first duty is to find the peace in you.

∗

You are peace personified.

∗

Even in the midst of a busy life, you can retain your peace. Learn to do that; then it will make no difference whether you are in a church or a stock market. Then it is only a matter of expanding that peace - it's limitless.

∗

Human minds create war. If we want peace, where should we begin? With the minds of the people. If the minds are changed, the world will be changed.

∗

Yoga believes in transforming the individual before transforming the world. Whatever change we want to happen outside should happen within. If you walk in peace and express that peace in your very life, others will see you and learn something.

∗

A mind free from all disturbance is Yoga.

PRAYER

Prayers are powerful, good thoughts.

✳

It is not the head that prays, it is the heart. A sincere prayer that comes from a faithful heart can perform miracles.

✳

The real prayer comes after you finish speaking.

✳

Your mind gets purified when you pray for others. You become a better person. Through your prayer you are expressing your faith in God.

✳

By praying for others, you get the benefit yourself, because you are opening up your own heart. You are showing your compassionate side.

✳

Sometimes your prayers are universal; in that case, those who have an open sail will catch it. But you can personalize it also, and it will certainly be received.

✳

If you pray for a particular individual, no matter where that individual is, your thought forms go there and reach that person.

✳

By your concentrated sincere prayer, you are
tuning your mental radio to receive the
omnipresent power of God.

✳

Sincerity in seeking comes only when you know
that you have a limited capacity. It's only
when you say, "I can't do it anymore, please
help me," that the help comes.

✳

God is ready to help you. Don't allow your
pride to get between you and God's help.

✳

When you pray, you send out healing vibrations
and good thoughts into the cosmos.

✳

The best form of healing is prayer.

✳

If you want to have a prayer, pray to God to
help you to always remember this Truth: that
you are God's child and God is taking care of
you every minute.

RELIGION

The purpose of any religion is to educate us about our spiritual unity.

✳

We are one in Spirit.

✳

If you follow the teachings of one individual, that doesn't mean that everyone should follow your teacher.

✳

The one and the same Spirit expresses itself in many forms and names to suit the age, time, and place. In one place the Spirit is called Jesus; in another place, Buddha; in another, Mohammed.

✳

There is no need to claim that only one form of God should be worshipped.

✳

The founders of the religions, the sages and the prophets who gave us these beautiful paths, want us all to be together.

✳

We have to do everything within our capacity to follow the principle that we should not and cannot divide ourselves in the name of God and religion, and to so educate others also.

Real unity means accepting all the various approaches, and that is what ecumenism means.

✳

God created all these differences for a reason. Our aim should be to understand the unity and enjoy the variety.

✳

Ultimately we all aim for the same truth while walking on different paths.

✳

Let us not fight in the name of religion.

✳

Stick to one path, but do not say to others that this is the only one. Recognize all other paths and respect them.

✳

The moment the understanding comes that essentially we are one appearing as many, all the other problems, physical and material, will be solved.

✳

All religions receive their light from the same source.

RIGHT ACTION

Whatever is presented to you, do it happily, joyfully. Everything is God's work. Do everything as an instrument in the hands of God.

∗

No action is undesirable as long as it produces a beneficial result to all concerned, including you.

∗

An action without any selfish expectation whatsoever is a right action. Such an act will never disturb your mind or body.

∗

The definition of a perfect act is one that neither hurts you, nor hurts anyone else. At the same time, it should bring at least some benefit to somebody.

∗

See that you bring peace and joy to everybody and no harm to anybody.

∗

If you died this minute, what would people be saying about you? If the majority of people would feel sorry about your departure, if they felt they had gotten a lot of help from you, then certainly God is happy with you.

Think of the golden present; sow what is
necessary, what is right. Sow good thoughts,
sow good deeds, and I am sure you will reap
good fruits. There is no question about it.

※

It is impossible to make a wrong decision. Even
if you make a wrong decision, you will very
soon know it is wrong and so you will learn a
good lesson.

※

Even if you make a mistake, it's for good,
because it teaches you that it's a mistake.

※

Your money should be very honest, clean money.
Then you will always be benefited by it.
It is not how much you earn, but <u>how</u> you earn it
that is important.

※

Failures are stepping stones to future success.

※

Let the whole world know by your example
that you are something beautiful and divine.
Let your actions bring out that cosmic beauty.

RIGHT THINKING

Don't be afraid of anything. <u>You</u> are eternal.

✳

Know that every minute that Great Presence is in you, functioning through you, and you are nothing but an instrument.

✳

Everybody has a heart. You should know how to touch it. Behave in such a way that you can transform other hearts, melt them.

✳

There is always a positive way of looking at things.

✳

The entire universe is a university. Everything and everybody is a professor to us.

✳

The basic reason for fear is the lack of knowledge of our true Self, which is imperishable, immortal.

✳

True knowledge is knowing how to use everything properly and for the benefit of all.

✳

Real freedom comes only when you know your true nature.

Know that you are already liberated. You are never bound. Thinking that you are bound is ignorance. As the pure Self, you are never bound. The true Self is eternally pure, unchanging, immortal, never tainted by anything. It is always peaceful.

✳

Anything that you call "yours" is not <u>you</u>. You are the passenger in the body, but not the body.

✳

Negate all you call yours and try to stand apart from these things. This aloofness is called Nirvana -- isolation of the psychological ego which is the basis of the mind.

✳

"As you think, so you become." Think well, you will be well. Think ill, you will be ill. It's all your thought.

✳

In our lives we should always think well. Train your eyes to see the bright side of everything.

SELFLESS SERVICE

Don't have any desires of your own. Whatever has to happen, let it happen through you.

✳

Be in the world; act selflessly.

✳

If you want peace, forget yourself. Think of the benefit of the others first.

✳

Put others first. Only then will you really find peace and joy.

✳

Giving brings harmony. Love and give; love and give. Think of the other person first. With this kind of attitude, the whole world will be a fantastic place.

✳

The real reward in doing things is seeing how many others will be benefited by them.

✳

Do things for the sake of others, not for yourself. That is the simple and practical way to find peace.

✳

Unless the human mind is freed from greed, jealousy and hatred, there will be more and more wars. If you free your own mind of all these problems, at least that little part of the world will be free from trouble.

✳

Divine Will has no tinge of selfishness.

✳

When you renounce your attachments, there is nothing to shake you. It is the feeling of possession, of clinging, that disturbs the mind.

✳

Dedicate your life in the name of God or humanity and your mind will always be clean and calm.

✳

Simply take it easy, trust in God, and do what you can. Let whatever you do be for the benefit of others. If you can, do something. If you cannot, accept it. Somebody else will do it; it is not that you have to do it all yourself.

✳

Serve one and all. Then you will have served God. Don't even lose a single opportunity to serve others. Serve, serve, serve, and you will find that you also are served.

✳

The dedicated ever enjoy supreme peace; therefore, live only to serve.

SPIRITUAL PRACTICE

The essence of Yoga and all the faiths and traditions is to be easeful in body, peaceful in mind, and useful in life.

✳

It is easy to sit and meditate. The most difficult part is to practice bearing insult and injury, learning to adapt, adjust and accommodate.

✳

Whether we want it or not, the world will give us the experiences we need and make us grow.

✳

Don't think that sadhana means only sitting and meditating. You can convert every action into spiritual practice.

✳

The very purpose of all your spiritual practice is to learn how to direct your thoughts and actions for a good purpose.

✳

Real spiritual experience brings harmony.

✳

We all want liberation. How to achieve it? You don't even need to do anything; just keep the company of the right people.

The aim of Yoga is to make the body healthy and the mind tranquil and pure. With a pure mind and a healthy body, you become a useful instrument for God.

*

Spiritual practice is not what you are doing, but what you are thinking.

*

Take it easy, but not lazy.

*

Do your best and leave the rest.

*

Stick to one path but respect other paths. Take the good from all others as a fulfillment of your own. Then your mind is one-pointed and you will progress.

*

If you believe in something, practice it in your own life. It is easy to quote scripture, but better to apply it in your life.

*

The three ingredients for success in spiritual practice are patience, devotion and faith.

SURRENDER

Free will means you are free to take
responsibility into your own hands or to give it
into the hands of God.

✳

God sent you here; He is working through you;
He has done today's job. He may use you
tomorrow. Be worryless, like a baby. Don't put
too much responsibility on your shoulders.

✳

Your only responsibility is to surrender yourself
into God's hands and allow Him to do
everything. That means allow the
Consciousness to function through you.

✳

Don't ever, ever put yourself down. You are
here for a purpose, and you are great in your
place. God has something for you to do; become
a humble instrument in His hands.

✳

We do nothing, nothing at all. That is plain
fact. None of us is doing anything by himself or
herself. There is a beautiful saying in the
Koran: "Without the Will of God, you cannot
even tie your shoelace."

✳

If you decide to put the weight on God's

shoulder, He is ready and willing to carry it.
You can decide to carry it yourself, but
ultimately, the whole weight is being carried
by Him.

✳

Even though individuals have their own will,
ultimately God's Will will win.

✳

If others cause us difficulty, we call them
negative people; but nobody can cause us
difficulty without God's Will. Those people
are simply acting as instruments of God.

✳

Know that you are being guided by God.
Whatever situation is presented to you is
presented by God. You should realize that and
surrender yourself in His hands. The true Chief
Administrator is God and no other authority.

✳

Even God cannot come and help you as long as
you have faith in your own strength. Complete
surrender means to give up totally and depend
entirely on God.

✳

Know that whatever task you do is God's task.
He is giving you the interest, the capacity and
the knowledge to do it. If you think of yourself
as an instrument in the hands of God, you will
always succeed in whatever you do.

THE REVEREND SRI SWAMI SATCHIDANANDA

The Reverend Sri Swami Satchidananda, a Master of Yoga and renowned spiritual teacher, is the author of many books, among them: <u>Integral Yoga Hatha</u>, <u>To Know Your Self</u>, and <u>Beyond Words</u>. He is also the subject of the biography, <u>Sri Swami Satchidananda: Apostle of Peace</u>.

He is the Founder and Spiritual Head of the worldwide Integral Yoga Institutes, and Advisor to the European and International Yoga Teachers Associations.

Sri Swamiji's universal vision is expressed in the form of numerous interfaith programs and worship services. He has been honored with the Martin Buber Award for Outstanding Service to Humanity, the title of Fellow of World Thanksgiving, Honorary Fellow of the World Vegetarian Congresses, Honorary Fellow of Concordia University, and the B'nai B'rith Anti-Defamation League Humanitarian Award.

Currently, he guides the development of a

large spiritual center, Satchidananda Ashram - Yogaville, in Virginia. The focal point of Yogaville is a unique ecumenical house of worship: LOTUS, the Light Of Truth Universal Shrine.